M
rEmedy
S
O
S
T
I
C

M
rEmedy
S
O
S
T
I
C

a compendium of mesostic poems
on the names of the 38 Bach flower remedies
composed by Alec Finlay

with contributions by Linda France

illustrated by Laurie Clark

Jupiter Artland
morning star
Ingleby Gallery
2008

naMes
makE
stemS
chOsen
wordS
Their
growIng
branChes

The 38 original remedies defined by Dr. Edward Bach (1886–1936) are a pharmacopeia of nature cure. Dr. Bach's philosophy of homeopathy highlighted the relationship between emotions or mental states and physical illnesses. I have composed a pair of mesostics for each remedy, to reflect the negative and positive characteristics he ascribed to them. The mesostic poem is an interleaved form, whose structure is suggestive of organic growth.

Alec Finlay

agrimony

Another
meetinG
anotheR
smIle
Masking
anOther
hiddeN
anxietY

A
praGmatic
wRy
grIn
disarMs
frOwns
aNd
worrY

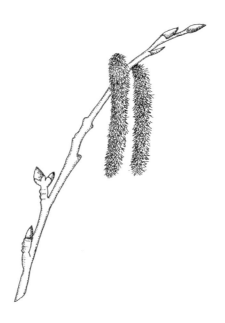

A
Sudden
Panic
strikEs
withiN

As
fearS
disapPear
lifE
sweeteNs

beech

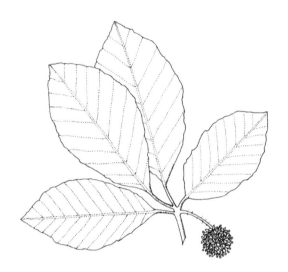

Becoming
wholE
wE
aCcept
otHers

Being
accEpted
wE
beCome
wHole

centaury

patienCe
wEars
thiN
evenTually
And
yoU
foRget
Yourself

doCile
friEnds
Need
Their
spAce
'yoUr'
Respecting
'mY'

cerato

Conviction
comEs
fRom
An
inTuition
prOven

reCognise
whEn
woRds
Are
jusT
Opinions

cherry plum

suiCidal
 tHoughts
arE
oveRwhelming
youR
 psYche

 dePression's
overwheLming
 yoUr
 Mind

suCh
overwHelming
tErrors
Require
youR
remedY

disPersing
Like
moUntain
Mist

chestnut bud

watCh

How

thE

diStant

pasT

goverNs

yoUr

presenT

Binding

yoU

rigiD

eaCh

Hurt

rEpeated

fixeS

patTerns

wouNding

yoU

furTher

unBind

yoUr

minD

chicory

eaCh
Hurt
Is
aCcounted
fOr
evERy
daY

Care
wHich
gIves
Caring
fOr
otheRs
selflesslY

clematis

Come
sLeep
thEn
dreaMs
hAzing
realiTy
In
cloudS

Cut

Loose

thE

soMbre

curtAins

That

blInd

uS

crab apple

superfiCial

    bRuises

    Are

    Blameless

    An

    imPerfection

accePted

    Loses

shamE

Clean

mirRors

Are

Beautiful

A

sPick-and-

sPan

Life's

impossiblE

elm

rEsponsibility
feeLs
overwhelMing

livE
Life
calMly

gentian

Gloomy
dEpression
turNs
lighT
Into
dArkest
Night

Give
mE
aNy
Task
I
cAn
uNdertake

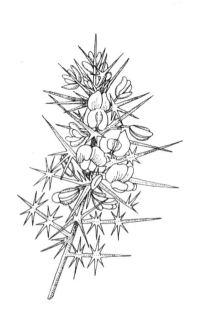

feelinG
hOw
eveRything
Seems
hopEless

Glinting
yOur
spaRkling
Self
aflamE

heather

tHeir

Ears

heAr

whaTever

tHeir

nEeds

Require

wHat
wE
shAre
Together
cHanges
thE
tRuth

holly

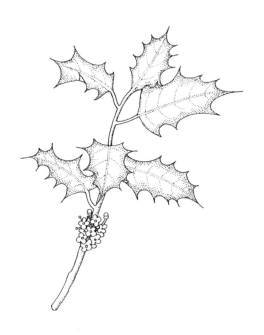

Hatred
Of
Love
fueLs
envY

tHey
fOund
Love's
peacefuL
mercY

honeysuckle

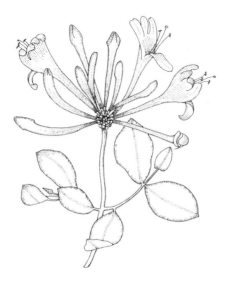

tHe
strOngest
experieNces
bEcome
memorY
kisSes
oUr
Consciousness
maKes
Last
forEver

tHe
mOst
inteNse
momEnts
staY
inSide
yoU
beComing
stucK
Like
skElfs

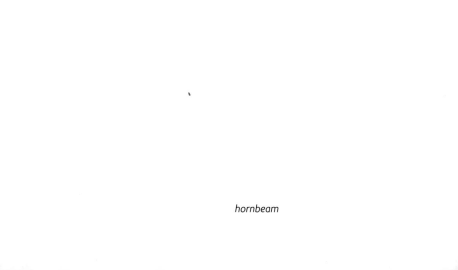

hornbeam

wHen
wOrk's
stRessful
theN
laBour
losEs
All
Meaning

wHen
wOrk's
caRefree
theN
laBour
dElights
plAyful
Minds

impatiens

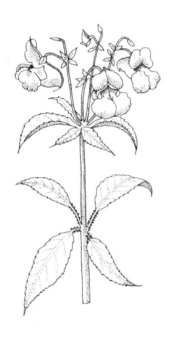

tweakIng

My

Plans

And

Twitching

fIngers

nErvously

arouNd

thumbS

thIs
seeMingly
imPossible
tAsk
isn'T
If
wE
doN't
ruSh

larch

faiLure
    Accrues
  oR
beComes
    Habitual

Life's
A
Risk
Come-on
tHen

mimulus

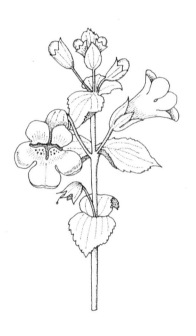

Me
knowIng
My
Understanding
wilL
cUre
thiS

Me
trustIng
Myself
yoU
Learning
yoU're
Safe

mustard

Melancholy
withoUt
cauSe
wiThout
pAuse
oR
remeDy

soMe
tranqUil
dayS
wiTh
A
Restful
frienD

despOndent
And
forsaKen

lOve
Anchors
Knowledge

One

Life

Is

giVen

suffEring

One
Life
Is
giVen
pEace

pine

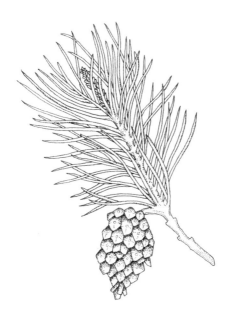

self-reProach

Is

stickiNg

nEedles

haPpy

In

kNowing

Enough

red chestnut

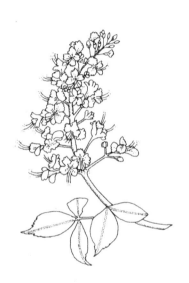

ouR
friEnds'
neeDs

eCho
tHe
vEry
needS
That
demaNd
oUr
aTtention

heR
frEtting
Diminishes

Calmly
Her
concErn
echoeS
The
momeNt's
aUthentic
Truth

rock rose

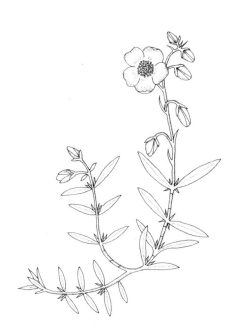

teRror
Or
shoCk
shaKes

thRough
Our
deepeSt
psychE

couRage
grOws
Courage
striKes

wheRever
One
perSon
Endures

rock water

Rivulets
strOke
Cold
rocKs

Water
weArs
Through
stonE's
stRength

Rickles

Of

Cast

rocK

floW

pAst

genTle

clEar

wateRs

scleranthus

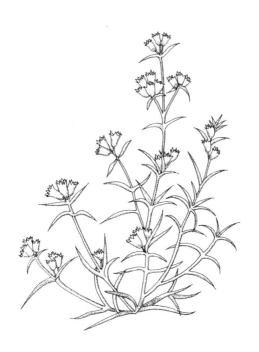

imposSible
Choices
Lead
mE
nowheRe
As
coNstantly
shifTing
tHoughts
Undermine
deciSions

pauSe
Consider
caLmly
lEtting
youR
cleAr
miNd
exTernalise
tHe
trUe
choiceS

star of bethlehem

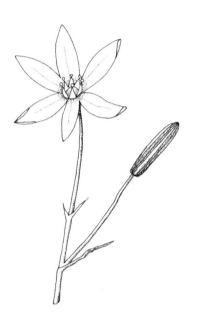

yearS
That
pAss
fuRl

Our
Feelings

But
deEp
wiThin
sHock's
stiLl
concEaled
wHere
no-onE
gliMpses

dayS
   The
heArt
unfuRls

disclOsing
   Feelings

   Buried
deEp
   Trapped
witHin
muscLes
   hEaled
witH
   rEscue
reMedy

sweet chestnut

Secrets

We

concEal

bEcome

sTuck

seCrets

tHat

arE

Shared

wiTh

someoNe

trUstworthy

unsTick

everyone'S

Worst

fEars

Exceed

deaTh

Come

sHare

Each

Secret

Terror

aNd

trUst

one-anoTher

vervain

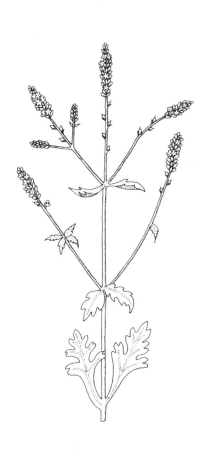

eVery
  Emotional
  Response
  Varies
  As
feelIngs
chaNge

eVery
mEntal
pRocess
reVeals
An
attItude
withiN

vine

eVerything

certaIn

caN

changE

eVeryone

Is

giveN

timE

walnut

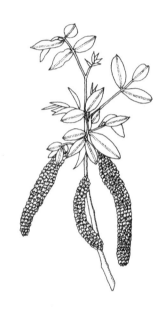

When
chAnging
bLossom
wheN
Unchanged
harvesT

We
Alone
wiLl
fiNally
cUt
knoTs

water violet

We

Are

waTer

wE

aRe

foreVer

flowIng

Or

fLoating

wE're

weT

draWn

towArds

Their

lonEly

natuRe

giVe

thIs

lOnely

souL

thEir

gifT

white chestnut

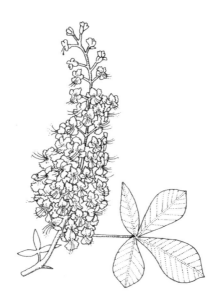

unWanted
tHoughts
persIst
wiThout
rEsolution

eaCh
nigHt
thE
wordS
That
weNt
Unsaid
repeaT

Whenever
tHose
nIght
Thoughts
rEturn

reCeive
tHe
fEar
Sense
The
healiNg
Undertone
wiThin

wild oat

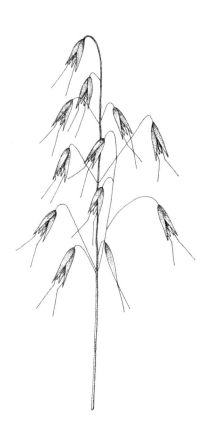

Whose

lIfe

Loses

Direction

whOse

gAins

limiT?

noW

I

finaLly

realiseD

Only

todAy

maTters

wild rose

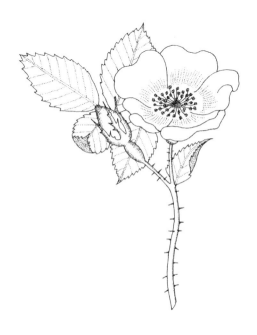

knoWing
wIldflowers
wiLl
faDe

whateveR
grOws
alSo
diEs

We're

thIs

aLive

wilDness

oR

sOmething

fadeS

insidE

willow

What's
hIdden
beLow
Leaves
nOw
shoWs

Who
Is
bLameless
bLaming
Others
Who?

notes

notes

Alec Finlay

372

Mesostic Remedy

Artist concept copyright Alec Finlay © 2008
Text copyright Alec Finlay © 2008
Drawings copyright Laurie Clark © 2008

Published in an edition of 750 copies

Designed by Alec Finlay and StudioLR
Printed and bound by Summerhall

With thanks to Alex Hodby and Linda France

ISBN 1-904477-06-2

www.alecfinlay.com
www.inglebygallery.com
www.jupiterartland.org